THE PRIEST WHO DEFIED THE KING

"Blessed are they who are persecuted for the sake of righteousness, for theirs is the kingdom of heaven".

Saint or Rebel?

Any profits from the sales of this publication are to be given to charities.

Revd. Vivian Enever

Msg. Brian Dazeley

Foreword

I am delighted to be able to recommend this booklet, but I do so in the knowledge that the Patron of this living of Newark is still the Queen of England. Let the reader understand – I have no wish to suffer a similar fate to that of Father Lytherland, parish priest of St Mary Magdalene Church in 1532 and the person behind the story! It is my experience that any exploration of our historical and theological 'roots' often create other kinds of 'routes' along which to travel – of conversation and encounter and companionship. I am pleased to have met the author and pray with him and many others that the unity of God's Church will be furthered by our common desire to work together.
Let the story unfold ...

The Revd, Vivian Enever,
Rector of Newark Parish Church
St Mary Magdalene, Sept 2007

Foreword

A few years ago we ended a parish mission by celebrating Mass in the fine Church of St Mary Magdalene. It was an extraordinary occasion and one of the most memorable days in my life as a priest. Just before Mass began the Rector stood up and simply said, 'Welcome Home.' It is quite clear that Father Vivian Enever and I both consider ourselves to be successors of Father Lytherland. I believe that this is significant, important, and deserves to be explored. I look forward to that. I too welcome this document and believe it will assist us as we continue to pray and work for the unity of Christ's Church.

Monsignor, Brian Dazeley,
Parish Priest of Newark's
Holy Trinity Catholic Church.

Preface

My Father and I spent many an enjoyable hour visiting old pre-Reformation churches, researching their history and searching for the architecture and art that once graced these beautiful places of worship. At Newark Parish Church not much remains from pre-Reformation days (apart from the building itself) of the treasurers and art that once filled this historic building, as much of this was removed during and after the Reformation. However, there is still the list of vicars, which hangs close to the west door and here we can read the names of all those who served the Parish Church of St. Mary Magdalene from the 12th century to the present.

The time of Reformation must have proved very difficult for all serving religious throughout England, torn between allegiance to the King and their faith. Some agreed to these changes and continued in their office, but for many, the break from Rome was too much to accept and knowing the dangers associated with protesting against, bravely chose to speak out, in the hope that the old faith might be kept. Father Henry Lytherland's name can be found on the list of Newark vicars, he was the last Catholic priest serving the parish church from 1532 to 1538. He attempted to resist the changes that were being made to his and England's faith. The accusation later brought against him (the funding of the Rebels) may have been a constructive means of finding him guilty of treason, so that he was executed, eliminating the vocal opposition of a well-educated and influential man.

This is now our history, but nevertheless, it is important that we remember those troubled times and those who were prepared to oppose the power of the King in defence of their beliefs and faith.

M. J. Carty

Contents

Page No

Introduction 9

The Thoughts of Father Lytherland From a Prison Cell in York Castle 1st August 1538

University and Early Days in the Priesthood 13

A New Leader in the Role of St. Peter 15

Destruction of the Monasteries 17

Time in Lincoln City 21

Brother Robert of Fountains Abbey 25

The Lincolnshire Rising and Pilgrimage of Grace 27

Charges Against Me 31

Walsingham 37

Prayers Together 39

Addendum 41

Points of interest 43

The Parish church of St. Mary Magdalene Newark
watercolour by Edward Joseph Towndrow

From the pulpit of this church Fr. Lytherland spoke out in defence of the old faith.

INTRODUCTION

Newark on Trent lies in the East Midlands of England, situated between the cities of Nottingham and Lincoln. Christianity may have been introduced to the Newark area by passing Roman soldiers, treading the route of the road they built. That road is known today as the Fosse Way (derived from the Latin word fossa meaning a ditch).

This Fosse Way links the cities of Exeter in the South West of England, to Lincoln fifteen miles from the town of Newark. Although the earliest known occupation of Newark was after the departure of the Romans in Anglo-Saxon times, the Fosse Way would have allowed foot soldiers and any existing local community to trade and to exchange views, including their religious beliefs.

In 601 Pope Gregory sent Paulinus, a monk from the same monastery as Augustine, with the second group of missionaries to England. While visiting the Newark district Paulinus assisted in the conversion of the local population, and at Newark itself multitudes followed him, some of whom were baptised in the River Trent. Paulinus built the first Christian church, made of wood in 627 at York. The church at York was later rebuilt of stone, and Paulinus also founded a stone church at Lincoln. In Saxon times a church once stood on the site of Newark's St. Mary Magdalene Parish Church. This church probably stood for the first hundred years after the Norman Conquest of 1066. At that time there may also have been a church where Newark Castle now stands.

In Saxon times England was divided into provinces including, Wessex, East Anglia, Northumbria and Mercia. Newark fell within the boundaries of Mercia. Each of these provinces was controlled by the nobility. In the early 11th century Newark was governed by Earl Leofric and his famous wife Lady

Godiva. Earl Leofric had amassed a fortune from the mutton trade around Shrewsbury and using his wealth funded the building of a monastery in the centre of Coventry in 1043. Both were generous benefactors to a number of religious establishments including those at Evesham, Worcester and Chester. In the 11th century on a high altar of Newark's Saxon Church, Leofric the Great of Mercia and his celebrated wife are said to have dedicated as an endowment the Manors of Newark and its church to the Benedictine monks of Stow, near Lincoln.

By the time of the Norman Conquest of 1066, under the authority of the Pope in Rome, a more or less unified Christian system of belief had been established in England. After the Norman Conquest the Newark endowment made by Leofric and Lady Godiva passed to the Bishop of Lincoln and in the 12th century this was then given to the Gilbertine Priory of St Catherine's, Lincoln.

The Gilbertine Order was founded by Gilbert (later Saint) of Sempringham, Lincolnshire, in the mid-12th century. It was the only monastic order founded in England. Holding the responsibility for St Mary Magdalene's Parish Church, Newark, the Prior of St Catherine's Lincoln, appointed the first vicar (parish priest), Walter de Coddington in 1301. Twenty-one appointments were then made up till the time of the Reformation, the last being Father Henry Lytherland in 1532.

Father Lytherland spoke out against King Henry VIII, in Newark Parish Church in 1534 and was critical of the enforced changes made to the faith that he had followed and which had been practised in England, for some nine hundred years. For that crime and for his alleged participation in the Pilgrimage of Grace he was prosecuted, found guilty of treason and imprisoned in York Castle to await his execution.

Let us consider the final days of Father Lytherland's life, as a prisoner awaiting the sentence of death. He may have reflected upon the events leading up to his trial at York and earlier, happier times, including his years as Parish Priest of St. Mary Magdalene, Newark on Trent, and days spent in the city of Lincoln:

The following is a brief account based upon historical fact, relating to the life of Father Henry Lytherland, St Mary Magdalene's last serving catholic priest.

GILBERTINE CANON

The Gilbertine monastic order of Lincoln held responsiblilty for Newark Church.

Note: In the following pages are mentioned some of the Acts of Parliament passed at the time of the Reformation. The Acts mentioned are:

The Act of Supremacy (1534):
An Act of Parliament declaring King Henry VIII 'the only supreme head on earth of the Church in England' a role formerly held by the Pope. Subjects, if commanded, were to swear an oath recognising the King's supremacy. People who refused to take the oath were later charged with treason.

The Act of Treason (1534):
An Act of Parliament making it treason, - punishable by death, to deny Royal Supremacy.

The Act of Suppression:
First Suppression Act (1536) - Parliament met in 1536, and by an Act of Parliament suppressed the smaller religious houses. This proposal gave rise to a long debate in the Lower House. Parliament passed the measure with great reluctance. In the preamble to this Act, Parliament was careful to hand the entire responsibility for the measure upon the King, and to declare that they took the truth of the charges against the good name of the religious, solely upon the King's "declaration" that he knew the charges to be true. In its final shape the first measure of suppression merely enacted that all religious houses not possessing an income of more than £ 200 a year should be given to the Crown.

University and Early Days in the Priesthood

'Academically I progressed well at school and at the age of fifteen I was selected to attend Oxford University. In my early years at Oxford I studied grammar, which included Latin and literature with rhetoric and logic and because I was studying for reception of Holy Orders, Theology. I read both civil and church law and in June 1516, after fourteen years at University, I was awarded a Bachelors degree in Canon Law. I remained at Oxford for a further five years and received a Doctorate in Canon Law, which was awarded on the 2nd July 1521.

My first employment was as a Vicar whilst still at University in 1514. At the age of 27, I became Vicar of Pattishall, Northamptonshire, a position held until 1529.

Whilst still serving the parish of Pattishall, a position at Lincoln became available. A Master Robert Newton, who had been the Keeper of the Altar of St. Peter at Lincoln Cathedral, offered his resignation in December 1521. The chapter of that cathedral assembled after vespers in the choir where my name was discussed for the vacated position. It was however, nearly a year after receiving my Doctorate and in June 1522, that the dean and chapter conferred the chantry and Keeper of the Altar of St. Peter on me. I gratefully accepted this role at the prestigious Lincoln Cathedral.

The title, Keeper of St Peter's Altar, carried with it responsibilities as the legal adviser to the bishop, dean and to the chapter (auditor et decidet causas et negocia quorum audicio spectat ad capitulum), on all issues that were of concern. St. Peter's altar stands in the southernmost chapel on the eastern side of the choir transept. I had become a chantry priest in my new role, with an annual income of £20 per year, whilst other chantry priests were paid only £5 to £6.

On occasions travel was required in serving the altar of St. Peter. An example of this was in July 1528, acting with legal jurisdiction, I visited the church of All Saints Derby, after the death of Master John Constable the Dean of Lincoln. I was commissioned by the sub-dean and chapter to conduct a visitation to this collegiate church and to report my findings.

Later in discussions held in the chapter-house, I was leased a property for 20 years, conveniently situated in the close opposite the south porch of the cathedral. This house was of great benefit to me during my time at Lincoln.

In addition to my work at the cathedral, in 1527 I was given the role, Chaplain at St. Mary's Melbourne, Derbyshire, and a couple of years later two more churches to administer. I was appointed vicar in the centre of Lincoln at the church of St. Peter at the Arches, less than a mile from the cathedral and vicar to the church in the village of Alkborough, North Lincolnshire. Attending my church at Alkborough meant a considerable time spent travelling away from the cathedral.

In 1532 after vacating my role as vicar to Alkborough, I became the rector of the nearby village of Belton on the Isle of Axeholme, Lincolnshire, and was appointed vicar to Newark by the Gilbertine Priory at Lincoln.'

A New Leader in the Role of St. Peter

'It was in 1534, two years after my arrival in Newark as vicar and through the government's Act of Supremacy, that the King declared himself Head of the Church in England. Shortly after followed the Act of Treason. Using this Act, anyone who opposed the King, and his self-appointment as head of the church, was charged with treason, as I am myself charged, with only hours remaining before my execution.

A couple of years ago the King ordered an investigation of every religious house and property owned by the church, including the church of St. Mary Magdalene at Newark. Monies once paid to the Pope were ordered to be given to the King. It was also decided to impose a ten per cent tax on income of the church, once earned from lands and property, money which had traditionally been used to support the clergy, the poor and for the repair and building of churches and other religious houses.

Government appointed Commissioners visited Newark and interviewed me on the value of the church's assets, after which they visited the Friary and the house belonging to our fifteen chantry priests in Appleton Gate. They even visited St. Leonard's Hospital Northgate and the Castle owned by the Bishop of Lincoln. I was commanded to give sworn testimony before these local commissioners as to my income as the parish priest, the lands, establishments owned and the revenues received from all sources. I believe the work of collecting this information was ordered to be completed before the end of May that year, 1535, the results of which were sent to London. We thought then, that this investigation for the purpose of valuation, might be followed by a seizure of our assets, but at that time I certainly did not envisage the destruction of the monasteries that has since happened. One can only hope and pray that the churches are safe from any such robbery. Many of the monastic buildings, their contents and associated lands had been given or bequeathed to the church by Kings and ordinary people. These gifts, as well as giving glory to God, had aided and supported the poor of the local community.'

FRANCISCAN FRIAR

The Observant Friars given residence in Newark by Henry Tudor then offered strong resistance to his son Henry VIII. Two of the Newark Friars were to die for their opposition.

Destruction of the Monasteries

'Two years ago, following the 'Act of Suppression,' the King moved forward with the dissolution of about four hundred smaller monasteries, those having a declared income of less than £200 per year, including of course our Friary at Newark. My friends the Observant Friars refused to swear the 'oath of obedience' to the King and his new Church and spoke out against it. They are consequently now without a home. It is said that no other religious order resisted Henry VIII with greater fearlessness and tenacity than the Observants. The Newark Observant Friars were, in the tradition of Greenwich and Richmond, loyal to Queen Catherine whom Henry VIII had cast off as his lawful wife. Three of the Newark Friars were thrown into the King's dungeons for their opposition and it is said that two, Hugh Payne and Brother Hayfield have since died from the appalling treatment they received whilst in the Marshalsea Gaol.

The Austin Friars who have had residence in Newark for a hundred years or so now live in the former home of the Observants. Many of the books once owned by the expelled friars have disappeared, together with statues and other sacred items. I remember seeing the will of my predecessor at Newark, Father John Smyth. He bequeathed a number of items to the Observant Friars including wheat and barley and twenty books. The Observants were learned men. Some had taught at the recently opened Magnus School in Appleton Gate, using the many books from their library. However, the lead roof still remains and the bell of the friary still tolls daily. In time, no doubt, the Austin Friars will be expelled and then the Friary will be stripped of its assets. These assets will then be sold and the Friary and associated lands, leased or sold, for the benefit of the King's exchequer or his friends, as has happened across Lincolnshire and the rest of the country.

My friend and Prior of the Gilbertine Order of St. Catherine Lincoln, William Griffiths, had been forced to watch the execution of his neighbours, the Abbots of Barling and Kirkstead, for resisting the King and the suppression of their houses. It was no surprise therefore, when I heard just two weeks ago, that William voluntarily surrendered the Priory of St. Catherine's, which by that time had held responsibility for Newark's Parish Church, since work began on its construction in the 12th century. It saddens me greatly to see so many of the beautiful monasteries of Lincolnshire looted, and razed to the ground, some say in retaliation for the role that the Lincolnshire people played in their brave resistance to the King two years ago.

It seems the dissolution of nearly four hundred of the smaller religious houses, over the last couple of years, was a great means of replenishing an exhausted exchequer and of removing the anticipated stiff monastic opposition to the proposed ecclesiastical changes. The King's triumph here is assured by the horrible deaths suffered by the monks, deaths secured on grounds of constructive treason.

There were several hundred monastic houses in England before the start of the destruction and these housed some several thousand monks and nuns. Besides these there were probably ten times that number of people dependent upon these religious houses from which they obtained a living in their service. These monasteries were considered to be the greatest bulwarks of the Papal system and the monks themselves were called "the great standing army of Rome." People were informed by government officials, "if the abbeys went down the King would never want taxes again" and this was a favourite argument used by Thomas Cranmer, Archbishop of Canterbury, who had been appointed by the King himself!'

Newark Friary

The former home of the Observant Friars.

At the time of the reformation the King collected treasures from the monastries and at Newark a chalice was taken, together with lead from the roof and a bell weighing 500 pounds.

Lincoln Cathedral circa 1536

Note: The close of houses bottom left, one of which would have been the residence of Fr. Lytherland and the Chapter House bottom right with the conical roof. It was here that the King's representatives gave the King's response to the Lincolnshire people after the Lincolnshire Rising.

Time in Lincoln City

'After serving Newark as a parish priest for four years, I was appointed as a prebendary for Lincoln. As a prebendary I had a shared responsibility for the administration of Lincoln's magnificent cathedral. It is said that this role is given as an honorary title to senior parish priests, so I was only too pleased to take on this additional responsibility.

What a beautiful cathedral we have at Lincoln and easily viewed from the monastic house of St Catherine's Lincoln, from which, as a canon, I had been appointed Vicar of Newark in 1532. Unfortunately the cathedral is not easily viewed from Newark, unless of course you were to climb the steps of the spire of St Mary Magdalene. However, the towers of the cathedral were always a welcome sight on my trips from Newark to Lincoln, once we had ridden or walked over the hill at Brough, on the many business trips made.

Whilst at Newark I still held the post of Legal Advisor at the Cathedral and later the post of Treasurer. In Lincoln, as previously indicated, I stayed in the house that had been leased to me, situated opposite the cathedral. Occasionally on my many journeys to the city, I would meet and walk with Father Edward Thomlynson, from Norton Disney, which is situated halfway between Newark and Lincoln. Two years ago, we celebrated Father Edward's thirty years as a priest, serving that village and attended a wonderful service at St.Catherine's in thanksgiving. Father Edward had been appointed Priest to Norton Disney by the Gilbertine Priory of Sempringham.

In July 1535 in the chapter-house, and on the authority of the bishop I was admitted to the dignity of the Treasurer. For this I had to take the oath of canonical obedience to the Dean and Chapter. On 13th July that year, after serving the altar of St. Peter for thirteen years, I resigned my title as chantry priest and legal advisor, allowing me to take on this new role.

My role as Treasurer was a prebend served from the church of Crackpool St. Mary, Lincoln. This responsibility was held from 1536 until my arrest. As a prebendary I had the honour of sitting in a seat at the back of the choir stalls known as prebendal stalls from which I could see and participate in the wonderful services held in that glorious building.

As a member of the chapter I would meet on a regular basis with others to discuss and decide upon the cathedral's business. In 1536 the chapter consisted of, amongst others, the Dean, Dr George Heneage, Precentor, James Mallet, Chancellor, Christopher Massingberd, Sub-dean, John Pryn and myself as Treasurer. As the Treasurer at Lincoln, I was officially charged with the maintenance of the plate and the vestments of the cathedral.

My friend and I, a fellow canon at Lincoln, James Mallet, would often enjoy long discussions in the cloisters after the chapter meeting had finished. At some chapter meetings there would only be a small representation of canons in attendance but at times, depending on the season, there might be as many as forty or more. Occasionally James and I were joined in our cloister discussions by the dean and the chancellor. Collectively as a group we were considered to be the principle officers of the cathedral and were called, as in other cathedrals, the Quattuor Personae, or the four dignitaries. We were all disturbed by what was happening in the country and especially by the destruction of the monasteries.

James Mallet is a Doctor of Divinity awarded by Christ College Cambridge and had held the position as the cathedral's precentor from 1532 until May 1537. As a precentor he arranged both the liturgy and the music at Lincoln. Born in Essex, in the Chelmsford area, he had the privilege because of his education, of mixing with royalty and was awarded the honour of Chaplain to the Queen Catherine. Although he had subscribed to the royal supremacy, signing the oath, it was very clear that the changes to the church made in recent years were very distasteful to him. He was presented by the Queen in 1514 to the position of Rector in Great Leighs, Essex and succeeded Wolsey (later the Cardinal), as a Canon at Windsor. He became Rector of the Parish of Leadenham, Lincolnshire and from Empringham, was appointed as a prebend to the cathedral.

Like myself, James has been outspoken at times and when it was dangerous to do so. It is said that Thomas Cromwell and his men are after him and that he is likely, if found, to be charged with treason. Unfortunately for James, he spoke out in the wrong company. When news came to us, of the great commotion made by the common people across the nation upon the dissolution of religious houses, James said, "Hath the King brought his hogs to a fair market?" His last appearance in the chapter was in May last year. Knowing his arrest was being sought he said his goodbyes and fled to Essex.'

Fountains Abbey

My fellow prisoner Brother Robert Morreby was apprehended at Fountains.

Brother Robert of Fountains Abbey

'I share my cell and sentence with a fellow prisoner Brother Robert Morreby, a monk from Fountains Abbey Yorkshire. Brother Robert was originally from one of the suppressed abbeys in Wales. After watching the destruction of his former monastic house, he was then expelled by the King's men and walked the considerable distance to join Fountains Abbey, a beautiful Cistercian monastery, much of which had been built in the twelfth century.

In our discussions, Brother Robert has informed me that the abbot of his monastic house of Fountains, William Thirsk, was arrested last year accused of joining the rebellion known as the Pilgrimage of Grace. For this, he and his friend Adam de Sedbergh, abbot of the nearby Jervaulx Abbey, were taken to London and hanged for treason at Tyburn. It appears that the Earl of Northumberland complained of the misconduct of the Abbot of Fountains for which the abbot was expelled from the monastery. Visiting Commissioners had accused the abbot of lacking faith and theft and they labelled him an idiot! Brother Robert says that he had known the abbot for eleven years since the abbot's election and that he was certainly no idiot, but a man of fidelity to his church and the Pope. According to Brother Robert the abbot was educated at Oxford where he graduated Bachelor of Divinity in 1523.

Brother Robert has been imprisoned here at York several weeks longer than myself and arrived here, I believe, in early May of this year. He had spoken out against the destruction of the old faith and of the monasteries, whilst sitting at the table with the late Abbot of Fountains and in the presence of Sir William Mallory. Mallory is one of the supporters of the King and the enforced changes, and shortly after sitting at the table with Brother Robert, had him apprehened, accused of treason for speaking against the Royal Supremacy'.

The Five Wounds of Christ

A design painted on banners carried during the Lincolnshire Rising of 1536 and then in Yorkshire during the Pilgrimage of Grace.

The Lincolnshire Rising and Pilgrimage of Grace

'In 1536 whilst in Lincoln, I was amazed to see so many gather in protest against the King's destruction of the monasteries, some estimated up to 40,000 people. This demonstration was later called the Lincolnshire Rising. I had hoped the King might listen to that peaceful protest and the requests made by his people.

By October 6th many had occupied Lincoln Cathedral, demanding the freedom to continue as practising Catholics and protection for the treasures of Lincolnshire churches. There was much work to be done, as it was decided to draft articles of grievance that were then to be sent to the King. Debates concerning the finishing touches put to this article moved to the Chapter House of the Cathedral. The official document once completed was sent to the Duke of Suffolk at Stamford. Copies were made of this document one of which was passed to Earl of Shrewsbury who at that time was in Newark, it is said that he passed this unopened directly to the King. The gentry were able to pacify the great crowds that had amassed some of whom had wanted to take direct action. Once the written grievances had been dispatched it was proposed the crowds wait their Kings response, it was suggested that to proceed at that time with further action might be considered treason.

It was in the chapter-house that the King's response in the form of a letter was later read out. Angry scenes followed, forcing us to escort the King's representatives through a south door, as crowds were gathering outside the main west door of the cathedral. The response stigmatised the county, as Henry described Lincolnshire as, "the most brute and beastly of the realm." So the response received by the people of Lincolnshire, to their requests for the return of their faith and the monasteries, was not what they had hoped for. Shortly after, when the crowds had dispersed, those leaders involved in this rising, including my fellow priest Father Thomas Kendall of Louth, were rounded up and executed.

Within weeks, another protest occurred in the North, known as the Pilgrimage of Grace. Throughout Yorkshire, Cumberland and Westmoreland, men of all classes, nobles, gentry, clergy, and ordinary people rose in defence of their faith. Over thirty thousand united in this spontaneous rising, which requested that, the Acts of Supremacy and Treason be revoked and that the Mass and the papal authority in England be restored and monks and nuns be allowed to return to their monastic houses. The suppression of the monasteries and other religious houses had brought social and economic chaos. For several centuries, monasteries had provided schools, hospitals, orphanages, shelter for the poor, employment for labourers and work for tenant farmers.

Robert Aske and the other leaders had written an oath for pilgrims. This bound them to take up Christ's cross, to defend the Catholic Church, to strive for the suppression of heretics and their heresies. This also required, strange as it might seem, that pilgrims swore to preserve the King. For this was intended to be a peaceful protest which with the popular support of the King's subjects would persuade his Majesty to reconsider his errors.

Pilgrims marched peacefully under their banners, on which were seen the five wounds of Christ, above a chalice and host. At Doncaster the pilgrims met with the King's representative the Duke of Norfolk, with his 8,000 troops. There were close to 35,000 pilgrims some of whom were armed, including 12,000 knights, squires, yeomen on horseback and 800 priests and monks. Norfolk accepted the pilgrims' terms and took them to the King. What else could he do? There was no violence showing that the true intention of the Pilgrims was only the peaceful restoration of the faith.

At a second meeting with the pilgrims in York in December 1536, Norfolk pledged in Henry's name, to grant a general pardon to all pilgrims and to hold a parliament within a year at York or Nottingham, to undo the disastrous legislation of the past seven years.

However, sometime later, acting in the King's name, Norfolk spread terror and devastation. In February last year, seventy-four men were hanged at Carlisle. In York, Hull, and Pontefract, some five hundred men were hanged, among them many monks and friars in their habits. Faced with another possible challenge to his authority the King arrested Aske, several of the leaders and others. All were convicted of treason and executed. Aske was hung in chains from the walls of a castle as a warning to other would-be rebels. Lord Hussey was found guilty as an accomplice in the insurrection of Lincolnshire and was executed at Lincoln. The loss of the leaders enabled the Duke of Norfolk to end the rising. Martial law was imposed upon the rebellious regions, finally quelling the insurgency. The pillage of the monasteries was therefore secured and could continue.'

On route to Tyburn

Three Carthusian Priors (dressed in white robes) and two priests (black robes) waiting to be tied to horse pulled hurdles, before being dragged from the Tower of London to Tyburn for their execution.

The three Carthusian Priors were, John Houghton, London Chaterhouse, Robert Lawrence, Beauvale, Nottinghamshire, and Augustine Webster of Axholme, North Lincolnshire.

Augustine Webster was the prior of the Carthusian House on the Isle of Axholme at the same time Father Henry Lytherland was rector of the nearby church at Belton, Isle of Axholme.

Charges Against Me

'Earler this year in Canterbury Cathedral and at the Tomb of St. Thomas Becket, a citation was read. This pronounced judgement on Thomas, the former Archbishop of Canterbury. It declared, as no one had appeared for him in his defence, that in his lifetime he disturbed the Realm and that his crimes were the cause of his death. Although the people hold him as a martyr, he is never to be named martyr, in the future. Thomas of Canterbury is one of the wealthiest and most famous shrines in Europe. The King has therefore summoned the dead archbishop to stand trial for high treason. The trial was held and the accused pronounced disobedient. Orders were given that his body was to be disinterred and publicly burned and the treasures of the shrine confiscated to the King.

Given that which has been ordered for Canterbury, I feared for our shrines at Lincoln. I have had the privilege of saying Mass alongside the Tomb of Lincoln's own Saint, Hugh. This is England's second largest shrine, a magnificent monument containing our Saint's relics. Lincoln has become the most celebrated centre of pilgrimage in the north of England. The shrine and its wealth presents a tempting bait to our King, as it is covered in gold, silver and precious stones.

As Treasurer at Lincoln in September 1536, I produced a list of all of the cathedral's treasures, given or bequeathed, representing the offerings of the piety and liberality of Kings and nobles, of saintly bishops and dignities, which had accumulated since the foundation of the cathedral. I estimated we had more than 2000 ounces of gold and 4000 ounces of silver and many precious stones on the shrine of St Hugh and covering the tomb of Bishop John Dalderby, who was popularly regarded a saint.

Knowing the orders given for the shrine at Canterbury, I foresee a similar destruction and robbery at Lincoln. I therefore, as Treasurer, let my displeasure be known to the chapter at the cathedral for this potential and intolerable sacrilege.

I cannot therefore deny, that I expressed views against policies introduced over the last couple of years. Policies designed by the King and his advisors to dismantle the English Church, which was formerly part of the Universal Church. Dismantle not only by introducing new legislation but also new religious doctrine. We have seen a number of Acts of Parliament passed over the last couple of years. In 1534 the Act of Supremacy proclaimed the King to be the only supreme head on earth of the Church in England, a role formerly held by the Pope. Subjects, if commanded, were to swear an oath recognizing this Act as well as the King's supremacy. The Act of Treason followed that year, making it treason to refuse acknowledging the King's position as head of the church, and this is now punishable by death.

My friend and Prior of Our Lady of Melwood Priory, Augustine Webster, refused to take the oath of allegiance proclaiming the King's position. Brother Augustine had introduced himself in the autumn of 1532 on my arrival as Rector of Belton, which is only a short walk from the monastery. He was educated at Cambridge University and became the Prior of the Carthusian house at Epworth, near Belton, a year before my arrival at the Isle of Axholme. On a visit to the London Charterhouse, he was arrested with others and imprisoned on the orders of Thomas Cromwell when they refused to take the Oath of Supremacy. When questioned on the royal supremacy they declared, they could neither assent nor so believe. For this crime Brother Webster and three others were hanged, beheaded and quartered at Tyburn on May 4, 1535.

Knowing the possible dangers associated with refusing to sign the oath I instead opted for an alternative, signing the document on 4th August 1534. This was also subscribed to by other members of the chapter and cathedral body, in all 72 signatures were given. I had hoped our King would, in time, see reason in the arguments put to him against the destruction of the faith by those who sacrificed their lives, including the King's personal friend Sir Thomas More. Sir Thomas was a renowned, scholar, lawyer, author and politician and rose to the highest position in England under Henry VIII as the Lord Chancellor. However, when called upon to chose between his faith and the King, he remained loyal to his faith and was executed as "the King's good servant but God's first." It seems however, that the King's advisors will stop at nothing to reach their objectives. Sir Thomas More was executed on 6th July 1535 for refusing to sign this oath of allegiance.

At Newark, against the new policies coming from London, I encouraged parishioners to continue their prayers to Our Lady. For centuries the English had held the Virgin Mary dear as the mother of Our Lord and now we have been ordered to remove such images from our churches. I preached that this was the work of heretics. I requested prayers for the King's council, as at no other time were prayers so needed and also requested my hearers to continue prayers for the dead and those in purgatory, against the King's new doctrine. In 1536, the Ten Articles were produced as the new church's faith. These articles referred to just three sacraments - baptism, penance and the Eucharist - rather than the seven. And then in 1537, the, 'Institution of a Christian Man,' known as the Bishop's Book was published. This book attempted to deal with the questions of purgatory, and the status of the four missing sacraments from the King's doctrine of the Ten Articles. The King had severed his country from ecclesiastical unity with the Pope, as the true guardian of divine law.

During the Pilgrimage of Grace, Norfolk had used Newark as a base and had moved from Newark to Doncaster with his 8,000 men.The Duke of Suffolk had also visited Newark and the King had urged that the town be fortified. So under the King's instructions the town and passages there and all bridges across the River Trent at Newark and Nottingham were secured. Newark remained awash with troops as another

Rising was feared and Newark was considered a means by which rebels might unite North and South. It had become very difficult therefore, as a priest, to continue with the practice of the Mass and other services that had been held in the parish church for some four hundred years prior to this catastrophe and before that time, in the Saxon churches of Newark.

I have been accused of two charges, speaking against the King as the new Head of the English Church and financing rebels who participated in the Pilgrimage of Grace in Yorkshire. The prosecution said that on the Isle called Crowle, men were well harnessed at my own cost. Both charges made against me are punishable by death, so speaking out as I did, against the changes to our religion provided sufficient grounds to enforce the death sentence upon me. In Newark Parish Church on Quinquagesima Sunday 1534, I advised my congregation against reading heretical books that contained anti papal rhetoric, which had recently arrived in the town.

They say highly derogatory sermons against the royal supremacy were preached from the Newark pulpit. I was aware that giving such sermons might later find me charged with treason but I was defending the truth. As the Vicar of Newark I spoke against the King, saying, because of his actions he was not a Christian. They also say, I reviled him with "many powde wordes" and that I spoke defending the Pope as the Head of the Universal Church.

Longland, Bishop of Lincoln, had sent round a letter to all parishes including mine at Newark. This was to be read at the time of Mass on the Sunday. This letter stated the jurisdiction of the Bishop of Rome was to be considered unlawful and extinct. Moreover, we were to see that schools taught this to their scholars and that necessary alterations were made in the service books. I naturally refused to obey the royal command and refused to use the new books of these Reformers, the so called new-learning.

I was arrested by John Horsely after I had concelebrated the 4 am daily Morrow Mass with my curate and two of the chantry priests in St. Mary Magdalene's Church Newark. I was bound and taken to York. On route another arrest was made of a gentleman called Thomas Mylnar who had been using the alias Lancastre. Horsely had boasted that he was now a rich man, for he was to be paid £100 by the King for our assured delivery to the York Assizes. A small fortune.

Evidence against myself, Brother Robert Morreby and Lancastre was handled by a Mr. Clarencieux. Lancastre argued his case rigorously and with dignity and composure, giving reasons why the prosecutions case was flawed. This only seemed to aggravate Mr. Clarencieux, who on giving verdict stated, "I devised that Lancastre's head should be set up by the body of Aske." Our fate had been decided before the trial.

Brother Robert has supported and encouraged me in shared prayers and in the face of death, a sacrifice we are both shortly to make. Just a decade ago England was in full communion with the Roman Pontiff and the Universal Church. Our King, once a great favourite of the Holy Father, had received the title "Defender of the Faith" for writing a book, 'Assertio Septem Sacramentorom,' against the errors of Luther and defending the seven Sacraments, the Mass and the Papacy itself! The same King who now forces his subjects, under pain of torture and death to reject what he had previously defended. I reflect also, that the Pope is the visible sign of Christ's Church on Earth.'

Our Lady of Walsingham.

This pre-Reformation statue sits above the south porch of St. Mary Magdalene parish church Newark.

Walsingham

'From all the parishes I have served, parishioners have made pilgrimages to Walsingham in Norfolk, to the Shrine of Our Lady. Many would call at Lincoln Cathedral on route and pray at the tomb of Saint Hugh. Back in the 1460s, a Newark gentleman left money for a priest from the town to make a pilgrimage by foot to Walsingham and Canterbury. The people of England have a great devotion to Our Lady. It was this land that was offered by a previous King, to the Holy Mother of God as her perpetual dowry 'the Dowry of Our Lady.' In fact several of our English Kings had been devotees of the Shrine of Our Lady of Walsingham, considered to be England's Nazareth. Edward I credited Our Lady with saving his life as a youth and paid homage. Others made pilgrimages including, Edward II, Richard II, Henry VI, Edward IV and King David of Scotland and even a French Queen, Isabella. Henry VII our current King's father, was a patron and praised Our Lady with his victory in the Battle of Stoke, fought close to my former home Newark, in 1487. It is now so difficult to comprehend, but our King himself made a pilgrimage to the shrine in January 1511, giving thanks for the birth of a son, Prince Henry. It is said he gave several valuable gifts and when he noticed that the windows of Our Lady's Chapel were unglazed, he gave the money needed to complete that work. There was no hint then of this impending disaster.

However, this King has stolen from the church and then sold what he has stolen. Several days ago, I heard that the King had the Shrine of Our Lady at Walsingham closed and the statue and all the jewels that had been given in honour and thanks to that shrine, removed and taken to London. Some say that the statue of Our Lady of Walsingham together with other statues from other shrines are to be destroyed by burning in public. It appears that King Henry is a man of great appetites. Besides his lust, his avarice got the better of him. Not content with just breaking from Rome and declaring himself the Head of the

Church in England, he will have access to the property and treasuries of all the churches and monasteries in the country.

When two years ago, our Queen Catherine died she was mourned by all of England. She had been banished from the court and was not allowed to see her only child during the last years of her life. It was said that on Queen Catherine's death the new Queen Anne rejoiced, for she was then truly a queen. Little did she know, that less than six months after Catherine's death, she would die upon the scaffold, accused of treason and adultery!

As the supreme head of the new Church of England, Henry, required all religious to sign an Act of Supremacy acknowledging his new role and renouncing the supremacy of the Pope. This new position made the King the actual owner of all the properties and treasuries of the church, convents, priories and monasteries. Many of the priors and my fellow canons signed the oath of loyalty to the King, I mentioned earlier the abbot of my former home the Gilbertines of Lincoln, but for many this was done under fear of death. To some of the heads of houses it seemed incredible that the old system was passing away forever, and they surrendered believing that their loss was only to be temporary

As we know not all succumbed and at Walsingham itself, in a field overlooking the village, the Sub-prior Nicholas Mileham, and George Guiseborough, a layman, were hanged, drawn and quartered on May 30 last year, for protesting against the changes taking place at the Priory.'

Prayers Together

'Up until the time of our trial, Brother Robert and I had been held in a very small, grey stone, dark, dank and foul smelling cell within the inner sanctum of the castle prison. After the trial and the guilty verdict we were marched from the adjacent assizes, loaded with irons the short distance across the castle grounds back to our prison. On route we could see Clifford's Tower high upon its grassy mound. Last year at Clifford's Tower, Robert Aske, leader of the Pilgrimage of Grace was executed on a specially erected scaffold. They say after his execution, he remained hanging in chains from the walls of this tower for weeks, as a warning to others. Since the guilty verdict we have been held in cells reserved for condemned prisoners. These are larger but certainly no more comfortable than those previously occupied; located on the corner of the prison we now have two windows from which we can see the castle's outer perimeter walls.

Earlier today I was visited by two gentlemen who made an inventory of my possessions and requested that I make a Will and Testament. I bequeathed twenty-six shillings and eight pence to Thomas Thorneton, my curate at Newark, for his assistance in managing the parish during my absences with the many other duties I undertook including those at the cathedral. Also to my curate at Belton a small sum and to my friend Agnes, I returned goods that she had kindly delivered to me at the parsonage at Belton. I bequeathed a small amount of money to Sir Roger Boull of Paulerspury, who made me feel so welcome at my first parish in Pattishall, Northamptonshire. To others I left money, including that for wages, to those who had served and assisted me in my duties as a priest. I signed my last Will and Testament with some considerable trepidation, knowing the agonising death that is to be my fate.

From my prison cell I have seen prisoners taken for execution to a place named Knavesmire just outside the city walls. These prisoners were transported in horse drawn carts, sitting on their own coffins, with the noose around their necks. But I am aware, as myself and Brother Robert are charged with treason, ours is to be a more humiliating and horrible death. We shall not be given a coffin, but dragged to the scaffold known as the York's Tyburn. We are to be hung and then, whilst still alive, lowered, bowelled and butchered into quarters. Our body parts are not to be buried in consecrated ground, but separated and buried apart. I pray to Our Lord for strength, a quick death and that I might see my Maker and my parents again shortly.

Brother Robert and I know the prayers and psalms of our daily office by heart, for us it is a complete daily and life cycle. In prayers at compline last night we said together:

Visita, quaesumus, Domine, habitationem istam, et omnes insidias inimici ab ea longe repelle: Angeli tui sancti habitent in ea, qui nos in pace custodiant; et benedictio tua sit super nos semper. Per Christum Dominum nostrum. Amen.

Visit, we beg Thee, O Lord, this dwelling, and drive from it all the snares of the enemy; let Thy holy Angels dwell herein to keep us in peace; and let Thy blessing be always upon us. Through Christ our Lord. Amen.

In the short time before my execution, I will pray for the people of the parishes I have served and for the Church and I hope that prayers for my soul might be offered for me in the future.

Deo Volente.'

ADDENDUM

Curriculum Vitae of Father Henry Lytherland

Father Henry Lytherland, a secular chaplain, was born around the year 1487. In his mid-teens (probably at the age of 15), in 1502, he was accepted into Oxford University and studied both civil and canon law, becoming a Bachelor of Canon Law on 30 June 1516, after 14 years of study.

Father Lytherland later became a Doctor of Canon Law at Oxford University on 2 July 1521 (at the age of 34).

- 1514 Vicar of Pattishall, Northants, exchanged 1529,
- 1522 Keeper of St Peter's altar in Lincoln Cathedral, vacated January 1535,
- 1527 Chaplain of St. Mary's chantry in Melbourne church, Derbyshire,
- 1529 Vicar of Alkborough, Lincolnshire, vacated January 1533,
- 1529 Vicar of St. Peter at Arches, Lincoln, vacated December 1533,
- 1532 Rector of Belton, Isle of Axholme, Lincolnshire, vacated on attainder,
- 1532 Vicar of Newark, Nottinghamshire vacated on attainder,
- 1535 Treasurer of Lincoln collated vacated on attainder, and
- 1536 Canon of Lincoln and Prebendary of Lincoln Cathedral from the church of Crackpole St. Mary

Lincoln, vacated on attainder (as a prebendary Fr. Lytherland had responsibility as a Treasurer for the plate and vestments at the cathedral).

Note: from above the word 'attainder' meaning charged with Treason.

Father Lytherland was reported by a local man Sir John Markham, for the sermons preached in Newark church in 1534, which were unfavourable to the King's supremacy. Sir John Markham had favour with the King and when the Friary in Newark was dissolved he later became the owner. Fr. Lytherland was also accused of being with the rebels in Yorkshire, and maintaining men at his own cost (1536). Father Lytherland was charged at York with Treason and executed either 1st or 2nd August 1538 (but most likely executed on the 2nd August, given that his Will and Testament was written on the 1st.)

On his execution in 1538, Father Lytherland would have been around 51 years of age.

(Source: AB Emden's 'Biographical Register of the University of Oxford 1501-1540 and Lincoln Cathedral Library)

Points of Interest
Father Lytherland and Lincoln Cathedral

It is described in the book written by A.F. Kendrick in 1928, 'The Cathedral Church of Lincoln' that, 'Harry Lytherland was the last treasurer of Lincoln. As he saw the last of the treasures carried away *(the dismantling of the Shrine of St. Hugh)*, he cried "ceasing the Treasure, so ceaseth the office of the Treasurer," and flinging down the keys on the pavement of the choir, he walked out of the church. This occurred on the 6th June 1540; Lytherland never sat in his stall again.'
We assume the date 1540, is incorrect, as Father Henry (Harry) Lytherland was executed in August 1538! Interesting nevertheless.

At the back of the choir stalls are positioned the prebendal stalls. These were installed in the 14th century. The actual seat that was used by Father Lytherland is therefore still in place. There is a prebendal stall marked Crackpole St. Mary!

Opposite the south eastern porch of the cathedral are a number of old houses. One of these properties may have been leased to Father Lytherland during his time at Lincoln.

The cells that once held Father Lytherland might be those to be found on the site of the York Castle Museum. These are in the basement of this building which was rebuilt a couple of hundred year ago, but it appears that the rebuilding project was on top of the original foundations and the actual prison cells. Also to be found at York, about one and half miles from the town centre, is the site where Father Lytherland was executed. This is situated on the York racecourse and is marked with a stone which simply reads 'tyburn.'

James Mallet (mentioned earlier in this booklet – see chapter, 'Time in Lincoln City') was Lincoln Cathedral's Precentor and a member of the cathedral's chapter at the same time as Father Lytherland. Of a similar age to Father Lytherland,

Father Mallet took a degree at Christ College Cambridge and in 1509 after nine years at University was awarded Bachelor of Divinity. He later became Doctor of Divinity. In 1504 he was appointed to the vicarage of Burnham Buckinghamshire, and in 1514 to the rectory of Lees magna Essex. He became canon of Windsor, and afterwards was promoted to the precentorship at Lincoln Cathedral. He was executed at Chelmsford in 1542. The alleged crime was that on hearing of the disturbances caused by the dissolution of monasteries, he said, "Then hath the king brought his hogs to a fair table." R.I.P.

Acknowledgements

Thanks to;

The Lincolnshire Archives Office and Nottinghamshire County Council for their assistance. In particular Mr Mark Dorrington the Principal Archivist of Nottingham County Council Libraries, Archives and Information Services, and all his Staff that provide those people interested in history with such an excellent service.

Dr. Nicholas Bennett, Lincoln Cathedral Librarian and Julie White, Assistant Cathedral Librarian for advice given.

Brother Ninian Arbuckle O.F.M. Archivist at the Franciscan Internal Study Centre, Canterbury, for information supplied on the Observant Friars of Newark.

Oxford University Archives for the time spent advising me on this subject matter.

The villages visited, Pattishall, Northamptonshire, Belton and Alkborough, North Lincolnshire, and Melbourne, Derbyshire, for making my visit to the churches that were once served by Fr Lytherland so enjoyable.

James Casey of Newark's Holy Trinity Parish church for his much valued contribution.

Christine O'Grady and Frank Goulding of Newark and Dr.Tony D'Mello, Nottingham for their editorial skills.

Joe Hubbard, Director of Wordprint Limited Newark For advice on publishing and for printing this publication.

Kevin Clayton for compiling this publication using his computer skills.

Thanks also is given to Fr. Vivian and Fr. Brian for their kind words.

Much of my reference material was found by reading the wonderful accounts written by one of the greatest history writers of Victorian times. Cornelius Brown wrote, The Annuals of Newark (1879) and A History of Newark in two volumes (1905 & 1907), and a number of other books (copies of which can be found in Newark Library).

Finally, I would like to give thanks to my Father, for spending time to share with me his knowledge and enthusiasm for the history of the English Catholic Church. And for the many wonderful hours spent visiting the pre-Reformation churches and monastic ruins that were found whilst exploring the English countryside together.